DECLUTTER YOUR MIND

22 SIMPLE HABITS TO DECLUTTER YOUR MIND & LIVE A HAPPIER, HEALTHIER AND STRESS-FREE LIFE

Disclaimer

The information herein is offered for informational purposes solely, and is universal as so. The presentation of the information is without contract or any type of guarantee assurance.

This document is geared towards providing exact and reliable information in regards to the topic and issue covered. The publication is sold with the idea that the publisher is not required to render accounting, officially permitted, or otherwise, qualified services. If advice is necessary, legal or professional, a practiced individual in the profession should be ordered.

From a Declaration of Principles which was accepted and approved equally by a Committee of the American Bar Association and a Committee of Publishers and Associations. In no way is it legal to reproduce, duplicate, or transmit any part of this document in either electronic means or in printed format. Recording of this publication is strictly prohibited and any storage of this document is not allowed unless with written permission from the publisher. All rights reserved.

The information provided herein is stated to be truthful and consistent, in that any liability, in terms of inattention or otherwise, by any usage or abuse of any policies, processes, or directions contained within is the solitary and utter responsibility of the recipient reader. Under no circumstances will any legal responsibility or blame be held against the author or publisher for any reparation, damages, or monetary loss due to the information herein, either directly or indirectly. Respective authors own all copyrights not held by the publisher. The trademarks that are used are without any consent, and the publication of the trademark is without permission or backing by the trademark owner. All trademarks and brands within this book are for clarifying purposes only and are the owned by the owners themselves, not affiliated with this document.

While all attempts have been made to verify the information provided in this publication, neither the author nor the publisher assumes any responsibility for omissions, errors, or contrary interpretations of the subject matter herein. Nothing in this book is a promise or guarantee (this includes all and any guarantees with regards to any results in the life of the reader and/or purchaser of this book, including earnings). Links to resources mentioned in this book may be affiliate links, meaning the author may receive compensation in case a product or service is purchased using such a link.

This book is for informational purposes only. The views expressed are opinions of the author alone, and must not be taken as expert advice, instruction or commands. The reader is solely responsible for his or her own actions. Neither the publisher nor any member of the author's team (including the author) assumes any liability or responsibility whatsoever on the behalf of the reader or the purchaser of this book.

INTRODUCTION

Thank you for purchasing this book! This book includes many simple and effective habits to help you in your journey towards decluttering your mind, and finding more peace, harmony, and joy in your day to day living.

<u>My primary intention is to serve you</u> through this book by giving you clear and useful information. My focus is on helping you achieve your goal of decluttering your mind and of providing a number of ways to help you feel happier by getting rid of negative thinking, anxiety, and stress in general.

One of the main things about this book is that it has useful and practical information. I have not included unnecessary fluff, as I value our time tremendously. There is no point in cluttering this book with hundreds of pages of useless information about topics not directly related to this book.

As a result, this book is filled with actionable tips and suggestions, and also useful explanation about the key concepts without being a 400-page book. To me, the point of writing a book about a specific topic is to provide the best information on that topic itself (even if that means that my book is smaller in size to other books out there). The main objective of my writing is to help my readers in the most effective way possible, rather than give them a massive book with generic information.

Also, **I have included real world examples** of what I have personally done over the years that helped me declutter my mind, and find peace and clarity in my thinking.

Additionally, **I have also included actionable tips to help you deal with anxiety, worry, stress, negative thinking and over thinking**.

Even if you do not practice all the habits listed in this book but start implementing a few of them, you will notice a positive difference in your life. You may also be encouraged to dive deeper into meditation or exercise. The important thing is that all of these techniques have many benefits, and have an overall positive impact on our lives in addition to decluttering our minds.

WHAT IS INCLUDED IN THIS BOOK?

22 EASY HABITS TO EASILY BRING MORE PEACE, CLARITY & HARMONY INTO YOUR LIFE

Ideas change lives. Think about it. It is the ideas that you came across and worked on that have had a massive impact in changing your life. I know mine has, and many of the best ideas that I have come across, have come to me through books.

This book includes 22 such ideas that you can make a part of your life. The fact is that **any** of these ideas can completely change your life for the better forever.

Personally, I have seen many benefits of having a clear mind, as our thoughts affect all areas of our lives on a daily basis. People who are cluttered in their thinking have a hard time with almost everything. They miss appointments, find it hard to make decisions, are usually confused and confuse others as well. I am not judging anyone who is cluttered in their thoughts, as I have been there myself.

Having been on both sides of the table, I can admit that taking the time to learn and practice the habits to declutter my mind has improved most (if not all) parts of my life.

Who will benefit from reading this book?

In my opinion, having a decluttered mind is a helpful topic and could be beneficial to everyone. With that being said, this book will especially help people who:

- Tend to think a lot

- Are stressed or tend to get stressed easily

- Feel anxious or worried often

- Have recurring negative thoughts

- Want to improve their overall health and wellbeing

- Want to learn ways to clear mental clutter

BENEFITS OF DECLUTTERING YOUR MIND

Before we get started with the various techniques that you could use to let go of the clutter in your mind, I would like to share with you some benefits that you are likely to experience as a result of practicing these techniques. Since I have been through this process myself (and continue to practice these techniques even now), I have greatly benefited from practicing the habits listed in this book.

There have been many ways that decluttering my thoughts and mind have helped me, and will do the same for you. Here are just a few of the benefits that I have experienced…

- o **Inner Peace** – Getting started on the journey of decluttering your thoughts and mind is one of the best things you can do for yourself and even the people in your life. When you are at peace within yourself and the world around you, life becomes much easier. There may still be things that challenge your peace of mind but once you have habits that help you to deal with those challenges, you will be able to work through whatever comes your way.

In my case, within a few months of starting a meditation practice, I noticed that my overall state of mind had improved. I noticed the things that would bother me in the past had lost their power over me and even though I still stressed about some of those things, they could not easily influence me anymore. I could easily get over them by using my meditation practice.

I do not have to tell anyone about the benefits of finding more peace internally. Everything, in general, started feeling much better for me, once I was regular in my practice of decluttering my mind. The best part is that now I know what to do to get the clutter out of my mind whenever it starts accumulating inside, and so feel a sense of security and control even when things seem to get challenging.

- o **Balance** – Since all our decisions are made in the mind, having calm and composed mind leads to more balance in our lives. You will find more balance by spending more time doing things that declutter your mind.

For me, having a mind with a high level of clarity and peace has resulted in increased balance in my life. This is a result that I did not plan to work for. As I kept practicing my meditation and other techniques to clear the clutter out of my mind, I realized that there was an increasing sense of balance in my life. I kept learning and implementing more ways to declutter my thoughts and mind over the years, once I saw the benefits of my practice.

o **Harmony** – You can expect to notice more harmony in your life as a direct result of getting rid of cluttered thoughts and mind. You will feel more harmonious in your relationships with the people in your life, more harmonious at your work, and other parts of your life.

Once I started finding more peace internally, most things in my life became more harmonious by themselves. The stuff in my life that was creating negativity and chaos did not resonate with me anymore, and I naturally steered away from it.

Let's Get Going...

I am sure that this book will give you new strategies, tips, and ideas that you can use to have a positive impact on your life.

You can use this information on a daily basis, and even make it a part of your lifestyle.

The main thing for you to do is to read this book, identify the strategies that resonate with you and then apply those strategies immediately. Applying this knowledge by taking action will make all the difference.

So, let's dive into the book now, and start this exciting journey...

TABLE OF CONTENTS

DECLUTTER YOUR MIND

In this book, there are many different habits to declutter your mind to ensure that you can find numerous ways that resonate with you. You do not have to do all of these but just implement the options that appeal the most to you.

Even if you pick only the options that you like and the ones which resonate most with your current lifestyle, you will see a massive positive change in your life.

CHAPTER 1

PROVEN WAY TO BE HAPPIER & HAVE A CLUTTER- FREE MIND

MEDITATION IS THE OPEN SECRET THAT BRINGS PEACE AND CALM INTO OUR MINDS AND LIVES

"Meditation can help us embrace our worries, our fear, our anger; and that is very healing. We let our own natural capacity of healing do the work."

Thich Nhat Hanh

Over thinking is quickly becoming the norm in our society, as the pace of modern life continues to increase. We are surrounded with automation and gadgets, and still, have to play catch up with everything that is happening around us. In addition to the increasingly fast pace of life, we have our pasts to deal with, the many things in our futures to worry about and maybe even some challenges to overcome in our present. No wonder, our thoughts and minds get filled with clutter easily and often.

Whether it is relationships, work or just keeping up with day to day life, it is becoming increasingly difficult for most people to keep up. What most people do not realize is that we are living in a world of extremes. There are too many choices, too many decisions to be made, too many things to look into, too many messages to answer, too many tasks to finish and so on.

One of the most effective ways to declutter our thoughts in this fast paced world is meditation. People have practiced and benefited from meditation for thousands of years, and there is a simple reason for that....it works!

My journey towards decluttering my thoughts and mind began with my practice of meditation. Many years ago, I would get stressed and worried easily and as a result feel negative emotions often. To overcome the negative thoughts and emotions that kept filling my mind, I started meditating. This one step towards meditation and decluttering my thoughts and mind has literally changed my entire life for the better.

What Is Meditation?

There are many definitions of meditation, depending on the type you are practicing; however, several forms of meditation focus on training your mind to be aware of the present moment and to pay complete attention to it.

Meditation is a practice of turning your attention inward and putting your attention on a single thought, breath, feeling or sensation.

How To Meditate?

Follow these steps, to get started with meditation:

    a. Find a quiet and comfortable room where you can practice meditation for 15 – 30 minutes at a time without being disturbed.

    b. Sit in a comfortable position.

c. Close your eyes, and focus on your breathing. You do not have to alter your breathing to make it deeper. Just breathe naturally, and put your full attention on it.

d. After a few breaths, you may notice your mind being distracted by thoughts. Do not worry or think that you are failing at meditation, when this happens. You can expect this to happen, as your thoughts have a lot of momentum.

e. Whenever you get distracted by thoughts, simply bring your attention back to your breathing. That is it. Keep bringing your attention back to your breathing. This is the practice of meditation.

It may take some time to focus your attention on your breathing for longer amounts of time. This is natural. The important thing is to practice daily without worrying about the results. By being disciplined in your practice, you will notice that you are able to focus on your breathing and meditate more easily.

This is the simplest form of meditation, and very popular for beginners. You can always learn about the different ways to meditate and practice the one that resonates with you.

In my opinion, meditation is the cornerstone for having a clear and focused mind. Having a daily meditation practice is one of the best things that you can do for having a peaceful and decluttered mind. This practice of meditation will also improve your overall health.

Benefits Of Meditation

- A study done by the University Of Massachusetts Medical School has demonstrated that meditation can enhance a person's overall brainpower.

- Meditation boosts productivity and promotes focus, according to a study conducted by the University of Washington.

- There have been other studies that have shown how meditation can improve the symptoms of anxiety and depression, help preserve the aging brain, and help with addiction.

- There is also a study published in Brain Research Bulletin that backs the claims that meditation can lead to reduction in stress.

- There are many studies (in the hundreds) published in various scientific journals showing that meditation, when practiced regularly, can be helpful in managing, preventing and coping with a variety of physical and mental health issues.

  These include:

  - anxiety
  - insomnia
  - depression
  - ADHD
  - asthma
  - chronic pain

There is also research that indicates meditation can help improve DNA repair and boost immunity.

Is Meditation Only For Religious People?

Many people think that meditation is a religious practice or for Buddhists and yogis only. This is not true. People all over the world, from all walks of life, are practicing and benefiting from meditation.

Even though there is a strong association of meditation with religion and spirituality, you can choose to view it as an exercise for your mind. Meditation is simply a practice, and anyone can do it without changing their religious views or beliefs.

The interesting thing is that meditation is widely practiced by elite athletes, biggest movie stars, musicians and even Wall

Street tycoons. In short, some of the most successful people on the planet also practice meditation. I have heard interviews of some of the most successful hedge fund managers saying that they meditate daily.

Also, some people think that meditation is odd or difficult, but it is actually fairly simple (that is the whole point, right ☺). Just like anything else, it takes a little bit of getting used to, and the key is to not get discouraged in the initial stages. If you keep practicing on a daily basis without getting discouraged, it will become an anchor for you.

When I started practicing meditation, I could barely sit still for a few minutes. Now, I practice meditation 2 to 3 times a day. It may only be for 10 minutes at a time but it has become an important part of my daily schedule because of the massive benefits I have seen as a result of practicing it.

"Meditation is painful in the beginning but it bestows immortal Bliss and supreme joy in the end." - **Swami Sivananda**

RECOMMENDED READING:

If you would like to learn more about meditation, the following 2 books are my picks.

a. My favorite book for decluttering the mind is **The Untethered Soul by Michael Singer**, who has been featured and interviewed by Oprah. This book is also a New York Times Bestseller with more than 1 Million copies sold.

The Untethered Soul is a must read for anyone interested in

decluttering their mind and thoughts.

b. **Real Happiness** is also a New York Times Bestseller and one of the best books on meditation.

CHAPTER 2

CLEAR YOUR MIND, BEAT STRESS & GET FIT

REGULAR PHYSICAL EXERCISE IMPROVES OUR HEALTH & HELPS CLEAR THE MIND

"I find if my body feels well and I exercise regularly, I think better, work better and feel better."

Helmut Jahn

One of the easiest ways to declutter your mind is to exercise daily. You do not have to be running marathons or spending hours doing intense cross fit routines every day. You can simply walk for 30 minutes a day and start enjoying the benefits of regular physical exercise.

Most of the highly successful people in the world exercise first thing in the morning, as they understand the power of exercising on their minds and bodies. I suggest you get started too if you are not already doing so.

You can pick the exercise of your choice. You can walk, join a gym for weight training, join a dance class, etc. I suggest you select a form of exercise that most resonates with you. This will ensure that you keep doing it daily, or at least a few times a week.

Exercising will also bring many other benefits to your life, in addition to helping you get rid of the clutter in your mind.

Benefits Of Exercising Regularly

a. **Weight Control** – One of the most common reasons that people exercise is to control their weight or to lose weight.

b. **Boosts Energy** – Exercising boosts our energy. You may have noticed that you feel more active and energetic right after a workout. This is counter-intuitive, and even though most people think that exercising would make them tired, that is not usually the case (unless one exercises too much).

c. **Improves Mood** – Exercising has a direct impact on our moods. Exercising can help boost the level of the "feel good" chemicals, endorphins and serotonin in our bodies.

d. **Brain Function** – An increasing number of people are beginning to recognize the importance of fitness for our brain. It is just as important as health for the body.

Workout leads to increased flow oxygen and blood to our brain which is very important for keeping it fit. Research studies reveal that working out improves memory and one's capability to learn new skills, at any age.

e. **Self-confidence** - Working out can enhance the way we look, which can boost our self-confidence. A big part of our self-image is tied to the way we look and as that improves, so does our self-confidence.

Some More Benefits Of Exercising Regularly:

f. Promotes Better Sleep

g. Strengthens Immune Function

h. Good For The Heart

As you can see, exercising is a good way to declutter your mind and improve your overall health at the same time. I highly recommend that you include a regular exercise practice in your daily schedule. By doing so, you will avoid the trap of procrastination, which is one of the most common reasons that people do not exercise.

I have set 6:30 P.M as time for my exercise daily. I stick to this time religiously and this one habit has made a big difference to my physical health. Also, following this routine is my way of de-stressing after work, and taking my focus away from work related thoughts.

My focus is on working out daily for 30 minutes a day. I do not focus on any result oriented goals but rather on just being extremely disciplined. You can try this out too, and see if it helps you. The main thing is to start an exercise routine, and then simply stick to it.

CHAPTER 3

AN EASY HABIT TO OVERCOME NEGATIVE THINKING

PRACTICE THE HABIT OF GRATITUDE TO BEAT NEGATIVE THINKING

"Happiness cannot be travelled to, owned, earned, worn or consumed. Happiness is the spiritual experience of living every minute with love, grace, and gratitude."

Denis Waitley

Being in a state of gratitude is a good way to let go of clutter in our heads and minds. Since our brain can think only one thought at any given moment, we cannot think grateful and unhappy thoughts at the same time.

By being grateful, we are proactively choosing to focus our attention on the blessings in our lives instead of what is thrown at us by our environment. This way we control our emotional state instead of our emotional states controlling us.

Counting the blessings in our lives is an age-old advice given by many wise people. Eckhart Tolle, author of The Power Of Now (a book definitely worth reading to help you in your practice of decluttering your mind) recommends this practice too. I have also heard Oprah saying that she has been keeping a gratitude journal for many years now.

How To Start A Gratitude Practice?

One of the best ways to start a gratitude practice is to keep a gratitude journal. Follow these simple steps to get started.

a. Get a journal especially for the purpose of writing down things that you are grateful for every day. By having a journal specifically for this purpose, you will have an uncluttered journal, one that does not have random notes in it.

b. Write down 5 – 10 things that you are grateful for. Do this on a daily basis. This practice should take only a few minutes of your time everyday and help you to focus on the blessings in your life.

You can write down more than 10 things if you would like to. There are days when I end up writing 15 – 20 things. I do not stop at 10. In fact, I write a minimum of 5 things but do not have a maximum number to stop at.

I write this list in the morning, most of the time. By doing this practice in the morning, I get into a positive state at the beginning of the day, which usually helps me stay positive throughout the day. You can do the same, and get a dose of positivity in the morning itself.

You can be grateful for anything, small or big. Do not think too much, just give thanks for anything you feel like. When I first started this practice, I was not sure what to write but now I give thanks for everything that feels good (including the food I eat, music I hear, beautiful weather, time I spend with my family and friends, etc.).

CHAPTER 4

HOW TO LET GO OF EXCESSIVE THINKING WITH EASE

BREATHE DEEPLY TO CALM THE MIND AND TO LET GO OF EXCESSIVE THINKING

"For breath is life, and if you breathe well you will live long on earth."

Sanskrit proverb

Breath is vital to life. It is the very first thing we do when we are born and the last thing we do before leaving from this life. It is estimated that during our lifetimes, we take approximately half a billion breaths.

What we might not recognize is that the mind, body, and breath are completely linked and affect each other. The way we breathe is influenced by the thoughts we think, and our thoughts and physiology can be directly impacted by our breath.

Deep breathing is often used to calm the mind, and can be a precious tool in helping to restore balance in the mind and body.

Scientists have actually documented the advantages of a regular practice of basic, deep breathing that include:

Lowered stress

Increased levels of energy

Reduced depression and anxiety

Muscle relaxation

Reduced feelings of stress and overwhelm

Most people are unaware of the impact of breathing on their emotional states. Breathing is an extremely powerful technique to control our mental and emotional states.

You may have noticed that our breathing patterns change with a change in our mental and emotional state, but may not know that we can control our mental and emotional states by proactively choosing the way we breathe.

By taking deep breaths, our bodies relax and minds become calmer. Breathing can have an instant effect on diffusing emotional energy, and thus is a great way to declutter our minds.

One of the most effective ways to let go of negative thoughts and emotions is through the practice of deep breathing. This focused deep breathing results in relaxing muscles, reducing your heart rate and calming the mind.

Deep breathing puts our attention back on the mind and body. We become more aware of what is going on inside our mind, as our mind becomes quiet. It is easier to become aware of the clutter and negativity in our thoughts when we breathe deeply.

By practicing deep breathing, we can let go of this cluttered thinking and gain more peace and harmony in our minds and lives.

The changes that occur physiologically as a result of deep breathing are referred to as the "relaxation response." The relaxation response is an expression that was first made by Dr. Herbert Benson. Dr. Benson describes the relaxation response as, "*a physical state of deep rest that changes the physical and emotional responses to stress... and the opposite of the fight or flight response.*"

Dr. Herbert Benson wrote a book called **'The Relaxation Response'**, in which he outlines the advantages of several relaxation techniques in treating a number of stress-related disorders.

Regular practice of deep breathing has numerous health benefits, in addition to decluttering the mind. Following are some of the benefits of deep breathing:

a. **Relieve Stress**

Deep breathing leads to a relaxation of our mind and body, which in turn leads to relieving any stress stored in the body. As we let go of the stress felt by us, we feel more relaxed.

b. Stabilize Blood Pressure (Or Even Lower It)

When we breathe deeply from our abdomen, it encourages a complete exchange of oxygen, which is the helpful trade of inbound oxygen for outgoing co2. This can result in the lowering (or stabilizing) high blood pressure.

c. Reduce Pain

Deep breathing brings in increased levels of oxygen to the body, which is needed by most cells in the body. The oxygen assists in removing the neurotransmitter within the blood and reduces pain that is caused by blood circulatory problems.

d. Increased Energy

The level of energy we have throughout the day depends on our breath to a large extent. The fuller our breath, the more energy we will have. By taking deep breaths, we get more oxygen into our bodies, which in turn increase the amount of energy we have.

How To Use Deep Breathing To Declutter Our Minds?

Follow these steps to establish a daily practice of deep breathing.

a. Decide a time of day that would be best for you to take 5 – 10 minutes to practice deep breathing. You can also add 5 minutes to your meditation time, and begin with 5 minutes of deep breathing. This will help your meditation practice, and you will not have to allot separate times to meditation and deep breathing.

b. Find a comfortable and quiet place where you could easily sit and practice deep breathing. You can leave your phone and other gadgets out of this room.

c. Sit in a comfortable position. You can sit anywhere (chair, floor, bed, etc.) or even lie down. Just make sure that you are in a comfortable position, and do not have to keep moving during your practice.

Many people think that it is not good to lie down, but I have found that it is okay to do so, as long as you do not fall asleep. If you find that by lying down, you feel drowsy or sleepy, then it is best to sit up during your practice.

d. Close your eyes, and breathe in deeply through your nose. Inhale as much as you can comfortably without overdoing it. Hold your breath for a couple of seconds.

e. Exhale slowly all the way. Hold your breath for a couple of seconds before taking your next breath.

Spend just 5 to 10 minutes daily breathing deeply, and focus your attention on your breath while you do this. This is a very helpful technique in taking your attention away from a racing mind.

If you notice that your attention goes towards your thoughts when you do this, simply bring your attention back to your breathing. Do not get upset or impatient, if this happens. Just keep bringing your attention back to your breathing and keep breathing deeply till you have done so for at least 5 minutes.

Another tip is to gradually increase the amount of time you practice deep breathing. You can get started with 5 minutes, and then keep increasing by a couple of minutes every other week till you can easily practice deep breathing for 15 to 20 minutes.

This practice is very effective for clearing your mind. Also, you should feel more relaxed within minutes of doing this practice.

What I like most about this technique is that you do not need to be in a special setting to do this. You can practice deep breathing in your car, in a park or while waiting for something, in addition to doing so at home. I usually do so whenever I find myself waiting...like at the barber shop or a doctor's clinic.

Keep in mind that a routine practice of deep breathing is one of the very best tools for improving your health and well-being. It is recommended that you practice deep breathing twice a day for at least 5 minutes at a time.

You can also use this technique to calm yourself any time you start feeling stressed or negative. By training your body with a regular practice of deep breathing, you will start to breathe better even without concentrating on it and will find it easy to declutter your thoughts with this simple technique.

"One way to break up any kind of tension is good deep breathing."

Byron Nelson

RECOMMENDED BOOKS:

Breathing: The Master Key to Self Healing by Dr. Andrew Weil. Dr. Andrew Weil says, "If I had to limit my advice on healthier living to just one tip, it would be simply to learn how to breathe correctly."

CHAPTER 5

FOLLOW THIS SIMPLE STRATEGY TO SOOTHE YOUR MIND

SPEND TIME IN NATURE OFTEN

"Keep close to Nature's heart... and break clear away, once in awhile, and climb a mountain or spend a week in the woods. Wash your spirit clean."

John Muir

A walk by the beach or in the park does wonders to soothe the mind and help us get away from our day to day activities. Spending more time in nature may also improve the way our brains work and improve our mental health, according to a study of the physical effects of visiting nature on the brain.

Since most people live in cities today, we do not end up spending much time in nature. Being away from the daily hustle has its perks, which may mean an increase in our mental peace.

Studies show that people who live in cities tend to have a higher risk of depression, anxiety and other mental illnesses as compared to people who live in smaller towns.

The events of people living in cities not spending much time in nature and having a higher risk of depression and anxiety seem to be related to some extent, according to an increasing body of research.

A variety of studies has found that urban dwellers with little access to green spaces have a higher rate of psychological trouble than people living close to parks. It is also found that city dwellers who visit and spend at least some time in nature have lower levels of stress hormones immediately afterward than people who have not recently been outside.

One of my favorite ways to declutter my mind is to go to the beach, and simply walk or sit. I make it a point to not listen to music or speak on the phone when I do this. The whole point of doing so is to not engaging my mind in the usual stuff but instead to take a breather from day to day things.

I have also noticed that when I use this strategy of just allowing myself to rest by spending time in nature without clogging my mind with thoughts of all the things I need to do that day, I usually get a lot of good ideas for my business. It is almost as if my mind frees up to let new ideas come in during this time. If this happens, I simply record my ideas in my phone and then work on them when I get back to my office.

This technique is very simple but effective. As a side benefit, you may get a bit of exercise too while walking along the water.

You can also choose to go to a park or go for a hike. Do whatever suits you most but the key is to get some quite time and unwind.

CHAPTER 6

LET GO OF OVERTHINKING WITH THIS SIMPLE TRICK

FOCUS ON WHAT COUNTS & LET GO OF THE REST

"The key to success is to focus our conscious mind on things we desire not things we fear."

Brian Tracy

We are bombarded with several tasks every single day. Our list of things that need to be done keeps getting longer. Rather than attempting to finish a massive list of items all by yourself, it is important to go through the list and drop all the items that do not add much value to your life.

Organize your 'to do' list in the order of importance, and then focus on completing the top 3 items every day. The benefits of this would be to handle all the important tasks first and also to get a sense of accomplishment.

It is important to question ourselves whether each task on our list is required. You can also look into delegating many routing items to a virtual assistant. This is one of the best ways to get more done without having to do everything.

RECOMMENDED READING:

15 Secrets Successful People Know About Time Management: The Productivity Habits of 7 Billionaires, 13 Olympic Athletes, 29 Straight-A Students, and 239 Entrepreneurs.

This is one of the best books on Time Management and letting go of clutter from your schedule.

CHAPTER 7

RELAX YOUR MIND & FEEL BETTER

TAKE TIME TO RELAX

"Rest provides fine-tuning for hearing God's messages amidst the static of life."

Sherry Miller

All of us need a break from the day to day running around, and moving from one task to another. It is better to schedule some rest time (even 15 – 30 minutes) every day rather than try to accomplish everything for the day, and then hope that we can get a chance to put our feet up and relax.

If possible, schedule this rest time in the afternoon or evening to give yourself a breather from everything else in your day. You can also join a meditation or a yoga class, which will motivate you to take this break.

Another thing that you can do is to just sit and relax during this rest time without having to do anything. Just sit in a comfortable and quiet space, close your eyes and relax.

If you get thoughts of all the things that need your attention, then just tell yourself that you will deal with these things after your rest break. This is your time to rest and let go, so make sure you get it in your schedule.

Many people think that they do not have time to relax, but in reality, rest and relaxation make us more productive. This is the reason why it is easier to get things accomplished in the morning. Getting a full night's rest gives us the energy and focus to accomplish our tasks.

Even though it may not be possible to take naps during the day, taking a short 15 to 20-minute break is usually enough to declutter our mind from constant thinking.

CHAPTER 8

HOW TO BE FREE OF WORRY & ANXIETY

LIVE IN THE NOW

"Realize deeply that the present moment is all you ever have. Make the Now the primary focus of your life."

Eckhart Tolle

Living in the now is an extremely powerful and profound piece of advice that has the power to completely transform our lives for the better.

Most of us are constantly thinking about the past or the future. We do this all day every day and miss out on life's precious

moments that happen in the now. By
focusing our attention and thoughts on the
now, as much as possible, we do not have to
deal with a million things.

You may have gone through some serious
challenges in the past that still haunt you,
or maybe you are worried about what may
or may not happen in the future. We all
have such thoughts that fill our minds.

By living in the now, we can usually deal
with whatever we face in the moment. This
practice of living in the present is
extremely effective because we stop
focusing on a million things and start
focusing on the one moment that counts the
most.

Once we drop the baggage of the past and
stop focusing too much on the future, our

minds become free of clutter and life becomes much more enjoyable.

You can start this practice by living just one day at a time, as being completely present in the moment at all times can seem like a daunting task. Just be present and live in the present, as much as you can.

When your mind gets pulled by thoughts of the past or future, and you notice this is happening, just bring your attention back to this moment by focusing on your breath.

Do not worry or get discouraged even if this happens often. Just keep bringing your attention back to the present moment, every time you notice that you are not present.

It takes a good amount of practice to keep coming back to the present moment, but I have to admit that it worth the effort. By living one day at a time, I am not worried about many of the things that may or may not happen in the future. Also, I am not stuck on all the things that have happened in the past but did not please me.

In The Power Of Now, Eckhart Tolle talks about the power of living in the present and explains how most of the thoughts that we think are about the past or the future. Eckhart also mentions that our minds seem to be obsessed with the future, and also keep dwelling on the things that did or did not happen in the past.

If you have read, The Power Of Now by Eckhart Tolle then you are already familiar with the notion of living in the moment, and the many benefits of this practice. If you have not yet read this book, then I highly recommend it. This book is single-handedly responsible for me letting go of the majority of the clutter in my mind. As a result, it has helped me tremendously in all areas of my life.

Even though living in the now is a very simple suggestion, it is extremely effective in simplifying our lives, and decluttering our minds. I suggest that you incorporate this mindset and practice into your life, and declutter your mind from negativity, worry, anxiety and stress.

CHAPTER 9

HOW TO RELEASE CHAOTIC THINKING & FIND MORE PEACE

KEEP A JOURNAL

"Your subconscious mind is trying to help you all the time. That's why I keep a journal - not for chatter but for mostly the images that flow into the mind or little ideas. I keep a running journal, and I have all of my life, so it's like your gold mine when you start writing."

Jim Harrison

Keeping a journal is helpful in getting more clarity in our thoughts. It is said that an average person has 50,000+ thoughts every day, which means that our minds are constantly thinking. To add to this excessive thinking, a big part of our thoughts can be random or chaotic, which leads to confusion and chaos in our lives.

One of the easiest ways to declutter our minds and to bring focus and clarity in our thinking is to put our thoughts down on paper by writing a journal. We have many thoughts floating in our heads, and when we put them down on paper, it becomes much easier to get clarity on a topic. By writing a journal, you may also find that there were many things on your mind which you were not even consciously aware of.

If you find yourself over thinking about anything, you can simply start writing your thoughts down. It is often beneficial to simply start writing a journal without editing or thinking too much about what you are writing. Once you have written down everything that was on your mind, go back to your journal and read what you have written. You will be amazed at the things that come out of you, and you will feel much better in the process.

CHAPTER 10

HOW TO DECLUTTER STRESSFUL THOUGHTS AND EMOTIONS

SCHEDULE TIME TO LET GO OF STRESS PROACTIVELY

"You need to be able to manage stress because hard times will come, and a positive outlook is what gets you through."

Marie Osmond

There are times when our minds are occupied by stress, worry or some other form of negativity and tension. We need to be clear and focused more so than ever in times like this but our minds usually go in overdrive.

If you are faced with a similar situation, then set some time aside to simply plan on how to deal with the situation at hand in the most effective way possible.

The key here is to not operate from a state of reaction but be proactive and schedule some time to think of all the solutions. When you do this, your mind will be focused on finding ways and solutions to handle your problem in the best possible manner.

CHAPTER 11

HOW TO FOCUS ON FUN & IMPROVE YOUR HEALTH

PLAY A SPORT TO KEEP HAVING FUN

"We don't stop playing because we grow old; we grow old because we stop playing."

George Bernard Shaw

Like other tips in this book that have several benefits in addition to letting go of the clutter in our minds, playing a sport has many advantages too. Playing a sport increases our social activity, improves physical health, can improve our ability to concentrate and focus, etc.

When we play anything, our attention is usually just focused on the sport itself. This is a good way to take a break from the day to day stuff in a fun way. It is also a good idea to include a group of friends, and make this into a group activity.

You can take up any sport you like but the key is to play the sport and to enjoy it rather than work hard at it or be overly competitive.

"Just play. Have fun. Enjoy the game."

Michael Jordan

CHAPTER 12

ENJOY YOUR WAY TO A CLEAR MIND

ENGAGE IN A HOBBY

"To be happy in life, develop at least four hobbies: one to bring you money, one to keep you healthy, one to bring you joy, and one to bring you peace."

Stan Jacobs

Just like playing a sport, engaging in a hobby directs our attention away from work and other responsibilities and towards an activity we enjoy. Pick any hobby that would be fun to engage in. You can even plan one evening of the week with friends who would enjoy the same activity.

Do you enjoy painting, photography, writing or making music? You can take up anything you like, and schedule at least 1 – 2 hours per week towards it. As you spend some time engaging in any activity that you enjoy, you will notice that your mind is not overly active during that time.

By engaging in activities that we enjoy, we are less likely to get cluttered in our thinking. These activities also help us release stressful or negative thoughts that may be clogging our minds.

CHAPTER 13

HOW TO FEEL GOOD EFFORTLESSLY

LAUGH OFTEN FOR A JOYFUL LIFE

"Laugh and the world laughs with you, snore and you sleep alone."

Anthony Burgess

Everyone knows that laughter is one of the best ways to de-stress. While running around from one thing to another, one can usually forget to take some time to enjoy small things and share a good laugh with loved ones.

Laughter has many benefits on our health and our lives in general. In her book, *A Better Brain at Any Age: The Holistic Way to Improve Your Memory, Reduce Stress, and Sharpen Your Wits*, Sondra Kornblatt writes about how laughter can make us feel better.

Benefits Of Laughter On Our Health:

- Triggers the release of endorphins, which are body's natural painkillers

- Increases oxygenation and vascular blood flow of the blood

- Lowers blood pressure

- Decreases stress hormones like cortisol and adrenaline

- Improves creativity, alertness, and memory

- Defends against respiratory infections

- Provides a workout to the respiratory, diaphragm and abdominal, leg, back and facial muscles.

You can include more laughter in your day by planning to watch funny shows and movies instead of watching random television shows. I personally watch stand up comedies often and love funny movies. You can find many standup comedy shows online, and on websites like Netflix, Hulu and others.

CHAPTER 14

HOW TO REDUCE STRESS & HAVE FUN AT THE SAME TIME

PRACTICE (OR LEARN TO PLAY) A MUSICAL INSTRUMENT TO REDUCE STRESS

"There's nothing - nothing - like the magic of playing music."

Butch Trucks

If you enjoy music and have always wanted to be able to play at least one instrument, then it may be time to take it up as a hobby. It is a good way to have fun, and learn a new skill at the same time. Playing a musical instrument can have a number of advantages in addition to decluttering the mind of unwanted thoughts.

Some other benefits of playing a musical instrument are:

- o **Reduction of stress** - Research shows that playing a musical instrument helps in reducing blood pressure and heart rate, which in turn reduces the cortisol (stress hormone), thus leading to us feeling relaxed.

  Michael Jolkovski, a psychologist that specializes in musicians, thinks that music also helps in reducing stress by helping people get connected with others.

- o **Improves Memory** – It has been found that music and memory go hand in hand. By learning to play a musical instrument, one makes use of both parts of the brain, which in turn boosts memory power.

Music education is also connected to higher IQ levels in addition to the physical development of various parts of the brain.

CHAPTER 15

WHAT TO DO WHEN NEGATIVITY STRIKES

LIST THE POSITIVES TO BEAT NEGATIVITY

"Positive thinking is more than just a tagline. It changes the way we behave. And I firmly believe that when I am positive, it not only makes me better, but it also makes those around me better."

Harvey Mackay

This strategy directly helps with releasing any negative thoughts that may be cluttering your mind. I have used this particular strategy often in the last few years (since I learned it), and have been amazed at its effectiveness.

Usually, when we start getting negative thoughts, we may get several negative thoughts one after the other until we break the flow. I call this phenomena 'going down a negative spiral'. It may start with a slightly negative thought but if we focus too much on it, we may get more and more negative thoughts with more intensity and pull.

Here are the steps you can take, when your mind gets filled negative thoughts, and you notice yourself 'going down the negative spiral':

o Stop and take 5 – 10 deep breaths

o Then, think of at least 3 positive attributes about the situation, event or person that you are getting negative thoughts about.

o Think of 3 more positive attributes about the same situation, event or person.

o Do this exercise till you have thought of or listed out as many positive attributes about the same situation, event or person.

REAL WORLD EXAMPLE: For a long time, I was working in a job that I did not like much. Initially, I was unhappy when I was working but I soon realized that my negativity about work was on my mind even when I was not working. This made me realize that I needed to declutter these negative thoughts about my job out of my mind.

One fine day on my way back from work while sitting in the train, I started writing down all the positives about my job...I wrote down things like "Having this job helps me put food on the table, support my family, gain valuable experience, make useful contacts in the industry, learn new skills, etc.

By the time I had to get off the train, I had several points on my list but the feeling I had about my job had completely changed. I was just feeling much better in general.

I have done this exercise many times since then, and have greatly benefited from it.

By doing these steps, you will have reframed your perspective on the topic that was negative in your mind and was making you feel bad. With a brand new perspective on the same topic, you will be able to let go of the negativity that was jamming your mind and causing unhappiness.

CHAPTER 16

HOW TO DEAL WITH WORRY

DELAY YOUR WORRIES & FIND A SOLUTION IN THE MEANTIME

"It's very important that we re-learn the art of resting and relaxing. Not only does it help prevent the onset of many illnesses that develop through chronic tension and worrying; it allows us to clear our minds, focus, and find creative solutions to problems."

Thich Nhat Hanh

Having the skills and ability to handle worry can prove to be extremely beneficial to anyone. In this method, you will learn to take control of your worry and respond to it with strength and composure.

When most people are faced with a worrisome situation, they tend to panic or start getting stressed out about a potentially negative outcome. I have been there myself, and know the feeling such a situation creates.

Next time you are faced with a worrisome situation, implement the following steps to help you deal with it.

a. Instead of 'going down the negative spiral' when worry starts creeping into your mind, put it aside for a day. (You can also put it aside for more than 1 day if the situation permits). The way to do this is to simply not engage in worrisome thoughts and make a decision that you will deal with all your worrisome thoughts about the situation after 1 day.

b. Think about the worst that can happen as a result of this situation. Write this down.

c. Then, write down all the ways you can respond if the worst happens.

d. Now, it's time to make one more list. Write down a list of all the ways you can turn this situation into a positive. Make as long a list as you can. Spend some time by yourself or include a family member or friend in this activity, and compile as long a list as you can.

REAL WORLD EXAMPLE: I lost my job during the banking crisis of 2008. One fine day, 2000 people were laid off from the bank that I was working for and I was one of them.

Initially, I was extremely shocked as it happened suddenly, and everything in my life changed in a matter of minutes. This was one of the most difficult times in my life, as I had never thought that something like this could happen. At this point, I had the choice to let the stress take over or to control my worries and stress proactively. I chose to do my best to be in control.

I remember coming home and meditating for a while just to release all the negative emotions that were coming up. That was a good first step in decluttering my thoughts.

Anyway, after that, I gave myself two days to figure things out and decided not to worry during that time.

After that, I wrote down what was the worst thing that could happen – not having money for rent was the worst thing at the time.

Then, I wrote down all the ways I could try to arrange for money for rent like getting another job, selling my car, selling other things I owned, borrowing money from a family member or a close friend, etc.

After that, I made a list of all the positives I could find in my situation. I wrote down things like...I could move to a warmer city and start fresh; I could look for jobs that I would enjoy more, etc.

By doing this exercise, I got a grip on my situation and felt more in control as I had a plan of action.

CHAPTER 17

HOW TO INCREASE YOUR FOCUS EASILY

PRACTICE MEDITATIVE LISTENING FOR FOCUS

"Listening is such a simple act. It requires us to be present, and that takes practice, but we don't have to do anything else. We don't have to advise, or coach, or sound wise. We just have to be willing to sit there and listen."

Margaret J. Wheatley

Most of us have heard of meditation but few may have ever heard of meditative listening. In fact, I stumbled upon this

realization myself and have never heard or
read about it anywhere.

So what do I mean by meditative listening?
I do not mean to simply listen to people
meditatively while speaking with them.
What I mean instead is a practice of
mindfully listening to soothing music for 15
– 20 minutes of your day.

Steps for meditative listening:

   a. Find some music that is soothing
      in nature. It could be instrumental
      music (listening to just a flute,
      piano, acoustic guitar). Any music
      will do, just make sure that it is
      something you like and is relaxing.

   b. Find a quiet space where you can
      spend 15 – 20 minutes without
      getting disturbed.

c. Play this music (you can make a playlist or put the song on repeat so you do not have to get up and select songs in the middle of your practice), and sit comfortably. You can sit on a chair, sofa, bed or on the floor. Just sit in a comfortable position wherever you are.

d. Now put your attention on the music that is playing. Do this without trying to focus too hard. Within a few minutes of doing this, you will begin to notice that your mind and body are more relaxed. You may also begin to breathe more deeply, as you do this practice.

When I did this practice for the first time, I noticed that I was feeling calmer and more relaxed within 10 minutes. The more I practiced listening to music in this way, the better I felt. I also started noticing that there were many subtleties in the music of the songs that I had never heard before, even though I heard listened to these songs many times.

I usually do this practice every night before sleeping, as it helps me unwind after a busy day and declutter my mind easily.

RECOMMENDED MUSIC FOR PRACTICE

Chakra Suite: Music for Meditation, Healing and Inner Peace

CHAPTER 18

HOW TO BREAK FREE FROM CLUTTERED THINKING

TAKE A NAP TO STOP CLUTTERED THINKING

"Sleep is the best meditation."

Dalai Lama

One of the simplest ways to declutter your mind is to just take a nap. Even a short nap can be very beneficial. By taking a nap when your mind is decluttered, you are giving your mind a break from the continuous flow of thoughts that may be cluttering your mind. This break allows the energy in the mind to settle down.

When we sleep, our thinking tends to slow
down and so we get relief from over
thinking or even negative thinking. You
may notice that your mind is more relaxed
after a nap. Being in a more relaxed state
after a nap, we can approach even
challenging things in our lives with energy
and a new perspective. This allows us to
focus on important tasks again with a clear
head.

There are scientists who are known to do
this. When they get tired of thinking too
much about different ways to solve a
problem but are unable to do so, they take
a nap and approach the same problem with
a different perspective.

Another interesting story and real world
example on this subject is of Matt
Mullenweg, the founder of WordPress
content management platform, which is

one of the most influential pieces of software on the Internet, running more than 19 percent of websites in the world.

Matt slept six times a day (for about 40 minutes each) with about 2.5 hours in between each nap. He says this was one of the most productive times of his life. Even though this is an extreme case, it goes to show that taking brief naps are helpful in clearing our heads and energizing our minds and bodies.

CHAPTER 19

HOW TO AVOID MENTAL CLUTTER

FOCUS ON DOING ONE THING AT A TIME

"Focus on the journey, not the destination. Joy is found not in finishing an activity but in doing it."

Greg Anderson

Most of us have too many things to do on a day to day basis. This is the reason we try to multi-task and work on multiple things at the same time. We try to get it all done, and this attitude often results in cluttering our minds.

Multi-tasking may not always be a good strategy, as it may result in having to re-do some of the things. If possible, it is better to simply focus on one thing at a time.

The point of doing tasks is not just to complete them while feeling stressed out throughout the process. It would be better to feel relaxed, positive and composed while doing the tasks that we do and to complete our work without any stress. What good would it be to complete our tasks at the cost of our health?

By focusing on one thing at a time, we can give our full attention to it, and operate from a place of relaxed composure. This practice also ensures that our work is of high quality, and needs little re-work. Most importantly, we avoid mental clutter from clogging our minds since we do not have to focus on too many things at the same time.

CHAPTER 20

A SIMPLE WAY TO STEER CLEAR OF NEGATIVE THINKING

CHOOSE HAPPY THOUGHTS

"The greatest weapon against stress is our ability to choose one thought over another."

William James

We have been taught a lot of things since we were kids but we have not been taught about some of the most important things in life. By this I mean, most people do not know that they can choose their thoughts rather than believe everything that pops up in their heads.

One of the most powerful ways to declutter our minds is to be aware that we have this power to choose our thoughts. I am not saying that we act as a gatekeeper to all the thousands of thoughts that come to us but I am saying that we can sit for some time during our day, and choose happy thoughts.

By devoting even 10 – 15 minutes per day to choosing happy thoughts, we are proactively putting our attention on things that make us happy. You can even write these thoughts down as a list if you would like. It would be good to have a list of things that make us happy at our disposal. Something we can pick up and read at any time.

By proactively choosing happy thoughts, we are making more space for happiness in our minds and decluttering the negative at the same time.

NOTE: The next 2 habits are Bonus Chapters from My Book 'Minimalistic Living'

CHAPTER 21

AVOID INFORMATION OVERLOAD

SPEND LESS TIME ONLINE

"The Internet is so big, so powerful and pointless that for some people it is a complete substitute for life."

Andrew Brown

Many people have become addicted to surfing the internet. The amount of information available to us online is staggering and is increasing very rapidly every day. With massive amounts of information and entertainment available to us on any topic and at all times, we have to be deliberate about our internet usage.

You might save many hours every week by staying away from excessive use of social media or forums and groups. You may also save yourself from being involved in unnecessary chatter online, which inevitably adds to our mind chatter.

Now that we have the internet on our smartphones, many people have become obsessed with their phones. Many people also have a fear of missing out on the latest news and trending topics. So they have a constant need for checking their social media accounts every few minutes.

According to researcher Dscout, the heaviest smartphone users touch (click, tap or swipe on) their phones 5,427 times a day. While the average user touches their smartphone 2,617 times a day. All of these touches do not mean going online, but even a percentage of this massive number shows that people have become obsessed with internet usage.

Since a lot of our internet usage can come in small quantities of simply picking the phone to check the news or check our social media accounts for new updates and so on, we may not realize the amount of total time being spent on these activities.

It is best to take appropriate steps to limit internet usage on a daily basis, in order to relax our minds. You can take the following steps to limit your internet usage.

- Get online only when you have some work, and then log off once you are done.

- If you plan to simply spend some time surfing without having any specific work, give yourself a time limit for doing so.

- Stay away from social media and news, at least one day of the week. This is a good idea during a weekend or time off.

It is not bad to use the internet, as it helps us with many things in our day to day life. Just be sure to minimize or avoid the clutter online to declutter your own mind.

CHAPTER 22

HOW TO PREVENT OVERWHELM

LIMIT YOUR T.V USAGE

"These days young kids don't have any place to form an epic adventure. It's more often in front of the TV screen or a laptop. That's very hard on them. They're being taught daily unsocial skills."

John Lydon

Watching hours of television on a daily basis adds to mind clutter at an alarming rate. We are constantly bombarded with information wherever we are, and by limiting the amount of television we watch, we can prevent an overload of information.

It is also amazing how much of the news is focused on the negative, and how many shows are not even entertaining anymore.

To counter this, you can only watch what you want to watch rather than sitting in front of whatever is going on at the moment. With streaming, you can watch shows, movies or news from your favorite sites, and can stop and play it whenever you want.

It is also advisable to cut down T.V time in general, which would allow you to get more time for important things in your life.

CONCLUSION

Congratulations on completing this book! We have covered a lot of practical information in this book. We have discussed many effective ways …from meditation to living in the now to declutter your mind.

Most people buy books but never end up completing it. They put off reading the book or even if they read it they never complete any of the exercises or go through any practice.

By practicing what you have learned here, you will start seeing results in a short span of time, and once you see positive results, you will be encouraged to keep implementing these strategies. It is imperative to not get discouraged in the process, and to keep practicing till you see the results you want.

I wish you much success in having a clutter free mind and life!

MORE BOOKS BY VIK CARTER

1. **EMPATH** - 16 Simple Habits To Protect Yourself, Feel Better & Enjoy Life Even If You Are A Highly Sensitive Person - Secrets To Thrive As An Empath

2. **MINIMALIST LIVING** - 33 Minimalist Lifestyle Habits To Declutter Your Home, Save Time And Money & Live A Meaningful Life - A Guide To Minimalism

3. **HOW TO TALK TO ANYONE ANYWHERE** – 23 Simple Tips To Talk To Anyone With Confidence, Start Conversations And Connect Instantly

THANK YOU!

THANK YOU for downloading my book! **I wrote this book with the intention of serving you.** So, if you enjoyed this book or found it to be useful, I would highly appreciate your feedback.

Please leave me your REVIEW on Amazon (no matter how short – even a few words or your STAR RATING would help ☺)

Your feedback is very important and will help me continue to write the kind of books that help you get results.

It has been a pleasure serving you and will keep doing so in the future.

Yours in friendship,

Vik Carter

Printed in Great Britain
by Amazon